the new dad

the new dad

from a to z real tips for a surreal time

Dan Consiglio

Andrews McMeel Publishing, LLC

Kansas City • Sydney • London

10 11 12 13 14 SDB 10 9 8 7 6 5 4 3 2 1

ISBN-13: 978-0-7407-9353-0
ISBN-10: 0-7407-9353-5

Library of Congress Control Number: 2009939463

www.andrewsmcmeel.com

ATTENTION: SCHOOLS AND BUSINESSES

Andrews McMeel books are available at quantity discounts with bulk purchase for educational, business, or sales promotional use. For information, please write to: Special Sales Department, Andrews McMeel Publishing, LLC, 1130 Walnut Street, Kansas City, Missouri 64106.

to **lauren**, **lily**, **lucy**, and **sam**.
for teaching **me**.

introduction

Parenting books can be frightening for expectant dads; I nearly had a panic attack two chapters into one of mine. I remember thinking two distinct things at the time: (1) *I can't possibly do all these things they're suggesting*, and (2) *Would I be a bad dad already if I set this down and watched the Cardinals' game?* The jury is still out.

But the point is, things don't have to be so complicated and scary. Most guys just want the straight dope from someone who's been there: "Will I ever sleep again?" "Will I be pooped on?" "What the hell is a Onesie?" You get the idea. That's why I wrote this book. Because when you break it down, parenthood is not as impossible as you might think. In fact, it's pretty fantastic.

is for anxiety.

If you're reading this, have a penis, and have a pregnant significant other or boarding pass in hand to fly to a distant foreign country to pick up a small carbon-based life form, you should be riddled with the stuff. That's the first thing to expect when you're expecting: to be scared shitless. Are you scared shitless? Congratulations. But remember, you were also really nervous the first time you got high and stole candy, and that turned out pretty cool.

b

is for breastfeeding.

It seems like such a wonderfully natural process: a brand-new baby searching instinctively for its mother's milk. How pure, how uncomplicated. And dogs make it look super easy. Fair warning: it will not be easy. After living in liquid for nine months, a toothless baby attempting to latch on to a dry nipple is like a dolphin playing a harmonica: there are lots of miscalculations and weird, guttural sounds. But when the little one manages to log on to the dairy server and establish that miraculous connection, it's truly an incredible sight to behold. Even if it does clearly signify the end of your co-ownership of your wife's breasts.

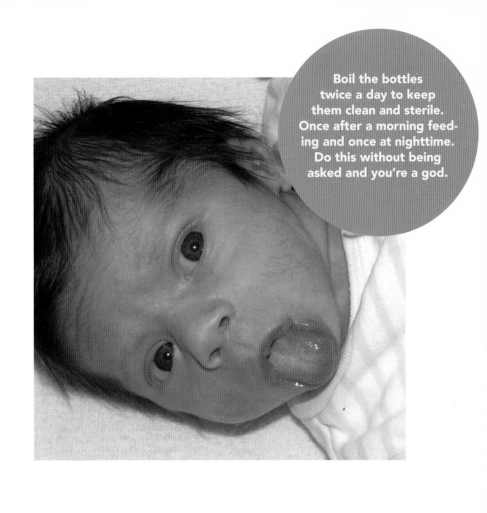

Boil the bottles twice a day to keep them clean and sterile. Once after a morning feeding and once at nighttime. Do this without being asked and you're a god.

If she's breastfeeding, she's probably been up all night. That means you get the 5:00 A.M. bottle feeding. No complaining. It gives her time to rest and you get time to bond. And watch dog shows on cable.

is for coffee.

You say you love coffee? You have no idea what it's like to love coffee. Not until you have kids. It's a whole different world. Until you have kids, you just like coffee. Are we cool on this?

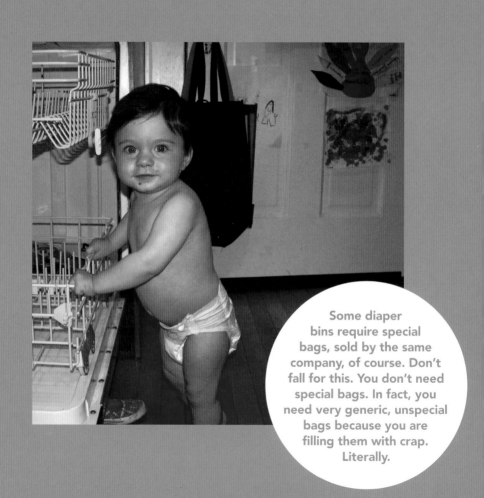

Some diaper bins require special bags, sold by the same company, of course. Don't fall for this. You don't need special bags. In fact, you need very generic, unspecial bags because you are filling them with crap. Literally.

is for diapers.

Most pending parents (OK, fathers) fear the soiled nappy more than lack of sleep, college tuition, or colic. True, they don't really know what colic is, so what's to worry about? There are even classes offered by hospitals specifically to help newbies learn the intricacies of "changing the baby." What a joke. It will take you exactly one diaper change to realize it's the easiest thing you'll do as a parent. The smell, however, could trigger a coroner's gag reflex. Breathe through your mouth and, whenever possible, ignore the full diaper until you can hand off the child to someone else. Then play dumb and claim that your allergies have you "all kinds of stuffed up."

Have your place spotless when she returns from the hospital. Yes, I know, you'll be in the hospital, too. So use your space-age phone to find and hire the best company in town. Multitasking is now a very real part of your life.

is for epidural.

Men don't beg and plead for four-inch-long shots in the spine. At least, men who aren't Chuck Norris don't. But that's exactly what your better half will do. After nine months of nausea, backaches, hip pain, heartburn, and hormones as inconsistent as the Mets of the nineties, she will ask anyone within earshot to stick her with a ginormous needle in her largest cluster of nerve endings. It's a beautiful ending to the miracle of pregnancy. And a final reminder that there is no way you could ever do this.

Make sure your computer, XBox, drum kit, whatever, is far away from her crib. Your amount of free time is directly related to her sleep. Both are key to your sanity.

is for free time.

You will have less of it. Far less. Shockingly less. But you will use it with force and focus. You will become a cyclone of productivity, a partially domesticated Tasmanian devil complete with whirlwind sound effect and wagging tongue. During your newborn's afternoon nap, you will cook, clean, write, phone, e-mail, spackle, paint, build, run, lift, and create absolutely lights-out photo albums worthy of national attention. Until the second kid comes along and then you just give up and snack.

is for gifts.

Accept them. From everyone. Birth announcements do more than announce the birth; they send a not-so-subtle message that in return for said announcement, you will be expecting some type of useful new baby thing, such as an ExerSaucer or Wii game console. Anyone on the mailing list bubble gets an announcement. You may feel a little awkward accepting all these gifts, but if your wedding taught you anything, it's that gifts are cool and you don't pay for them.

Load up on batteries now. Nearly every swing, bouncy seat, and baby toy requires, but does not come with, batteries. Forget the Quik Stop. Go directly to the nearest wholesale club for a value pack of one million.

is for help.

You are not expected to be Superman and Supermom. Know when to ask for help and don't be ashamed to do so. Here's a helpful guide: If you pour steaming coffee into his bottle, it's time to ask for help. If you take Baby for a drive to tire him out and you fall asleep, it's time to ask for help. If you cry watching Baby Einstein videos, it's time to seek immediate psychiatric care.

Live near a college? Then you live near good babysitters. Try for nursing students; most are responsible women who know crucial life-saving skills. Many sororities have babysitting networks, but please, let your wife make that call.

is for important.

There have been moments in your life that have made you feel all grown up. I'm not talking about the symphony of bone cracks, whizzes, and pops that accompany your morning stretch; I mean in a good way. Your first quote in a newspaper, for example. Or that time you told your mom to "mind her own business" in front of your smiling wife. But having a child transcends all that. Having a child makes you feel *important*. Cradling your seconds-old baby in your arms clarifies your role on this planet like nothing else. But be warned, not everyone finds you so important. Hot women will continue to ignore you, which is just fine; you don't need that kind of pressure right now.

Don't expect instant feedback. But that doesn't mean you and Baby can't communicate. Talk, laugh, smile. Try this: Stick your tongue out. In a few weeks, she'll stick hers out, too. And then you'll cry. You big baby.

Take him with you. OK, not to happy hour, but to brunch the next morning or dinner on Saturday night. He'll sleep, and you can get out of the house. Trust me, you won't miss the tequila shots.

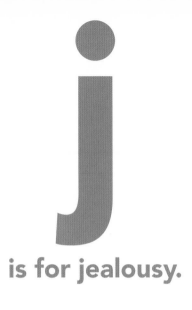

is for jealousy.

Maybe you're not the jealous type, but when five o'clock on Friday rolls around and the boys from work are headed for delicious beer and you're headed to the 5:15 diaper-change express, it will hit you. When you walk in the door and your spit-up-soaked wife hands you a crying baby, it will hit you harder. But when that baby smiles at you, Daddy, it will absolutely flatten you like a cartoon anvil of joy. Even though it was just gas, and not really a smile.

It might take a while for things to get back to normal in the boudoir. Don't be alarmed. To move things along, try a back rub. New moms love those. Or give her a bath. And clean yourself up, too, Don Juan.

is for kiss.

As you've undoubtedly been told, a lot changes after you have a baby. But perhaps people have failed to mention one important shift: the shift from a pre- to postbaby kiss with your spouse. It's not hard, in fact; just the opposite. Both parties simply purse their lips together and lean in for a nice, efficient peck—no tongues, no additional contact. It's the perfect way to say, "I love you; I'm just not interested in touching you right now." IMPORTANT: Respect the postbaby kiss. Your spouse will inform you when regular business can resume.

The mixed tape returns. They worked for old girlfriends; how about for your daughter? Burn a special CD for the two of you to listen to before bedtime. Introduce her to R.E.M., maybe a little Smiths. But not too much Smiths.

is for love.

In the hopefully helpful-yet-never-preachy spirit of this book, let me just say: you have no idea what love is. Not until you have a child, that is. I'm not so sure it's PC to suggest that the childless will never know real love, but wow is it true. You're too freaked out to realize the depth of this new love the first time you hold your little one, but wait a week. Bring her home. Sing to her. Watch her sleep. You won't be able to imagine your life without her. No matter what anyone says, humans are not capable of feeling this way about cars or crown molding.

is for movies.

Do you go to a lot of movies? Good for you. That's going to change.

Rent shows, not movies, at first. You'll be lucky to get two-hour increments of peace and consciousness, but you can knock off two episodes of *Weeds* on a Friday night, no problem.

is for network.

Freemasons, Shriners, Latinos, these groups have nothing on the instant camaraderie and shared experience between new parents. The transformation is swift and complete. Within days of the birth of your child, the person who refuses to acknowledge the presence of other human life on airplanes (you) will strike up animated conversations with anyone pushing a stroller. And they'll be thrilled to oblige; total strangers will happily describe to you the condition of their wife's breasts in shocking detail. The great thing is, now that you have kids, this passes as an adult conversation. Awesome.

Babies' limbs are like Twizzlers; they go every which way. And they kick like Pelé on the changing table. Hang a mobile over the table to capture Baby's attention. Then cram him into that Onesie like a stuffed turkey.

is for Onesies.

Pronounced wun-zeez, these are the cute little one-piece jumpsuits your baby wears. They come in lots of adorable patterns like fuzzy bunnies and turtles holding balloons. *Turtles holding balloons*—just imagine! When you finally decide which delightful outfit you'd like little Jerry to sport over to NaNa's house, good luck cramming him into it. Imagine a gentle yet retarded bear wrestling with an uninterested mouse. That's what dressing your newborn is like. You are the gentle yet retarded bear.

Men don't scrapbook, but there are a ton of Web sites where you can create incredible hardbound photo books from your pics. Just upload them and select a layout. The books arrive on your doorstep in no time.

is for pictures.

You'll take thousands. Even if the only photos you've taken to this point are from "that one kick-ass float trip with Kansas City Derek," you'll click away at your child daily like a sports photographer on Jolt Cola. Remember Jolt Cola? Anyhoo, you'll want to invest in a badass digital camera, one with twelve megapahoozles, at least. And just a word of advice: Let your significant other pose the child, as painful as it may seem. She carried her for nine months, she can prop her up like a loaf of bread in a beret if she wants.

White noise is beautiful. Get a CD of nature sounds for his room. Keep the volume low and play it every day at nap and bedtime. You won't have to tiptoe and whisper, and Baby gets a nice little concert.

is for quiet.

You will have a new definition of quiet. Before Baby, movies were surround-sound sensory assaults, ringtones serenaded from the other side of the apartment, and kitchen appliances were rocked with reckless abandon. After Baby, a ticking clock sounds like a Dokken show. Everything's amplified by one million when he naps. You'll curse the mailman and glare menacingly at garbage trucks like a senior citizen on a Rascal. You'll dive on ringing phones like a war hero on a live grenade. It's embarrassing. But if it'll buy you another fifteen minutes of golden silence, you'll do it. Just wait.

Babies make great audiences— for short performances. Sing, juggle, work on that standup routine—anything to capture their attention. But be warned, they make for a tough crowd: very little smiling and lots of gas.

is for repetition.

Babies learn through repetition. Daddies lose their freaking minds through repetition. See the problem? Thirty rounds of peekaboo may not be enough for your little buddy, but you know how this game works and you know you can't win. So what's in it for Dad? Simple: Your son likes it. A lot. Hey, it's really no different than you and your friends quoting *Caddyshack* for the last twenty years. You do it as long as it works. Like father, like son.

s

is for sweat.

Because you will sweat. You will discover vast, untapped personal sweat reservoirs. When your four-month-old begins to scream uncontrollably in the middle of a cramped, airless flight to some joyless destination such as Columbus, and you can literally feel the shameful, disapproving look from the old bag in 32C (because you will never be allowed anywhere near the front of the plane with little children), the sweat will flow like the confluence of two great rivers, heretofore meandering, now united with the surging power of *purpose*. But you get over it. In fact, you learn to enjoy pissing off the back of the plane.

Feed the little nipper on takeoff. The swallowing will help keep his ears from popping. And it might just instigate a little nap. When he wakes up, thrust no less than twelve toys in his face.

is for tired.

It's true. Babies cry, and often in the middle of the night. Newborns can sleep up to twenty hours per day yet you'd swear over your fifth cup of coffee that you've sired the world's smallest vampire. So yes, all the annoying warnings you get from new parents about the lack of sleep may be true, but does that mean they should be allowed to keep touching your arm like that? Of course not. Listen, it's not so bad. Make simple adjustments: go to bed instead of having that next beer, only watch *one* *SportsCenter*, stop flossing. Get your sleep when you can and you'll be fine. Unless you're a mom; then you're royally screwed.

Catnap like a fiend. Snuggle up to Baby right as he's about to drift off. Trust me, no one will disturb a father dozing next to his newborn; it's just too cute. Get your timing right and you might get seven naps a day.

Boxers or briefs? Boxer briefs. These ultracomfy under-garments fit parenthood to a T. When Baby is asleep in your arms, you can't move to adjust your shorts. And they nearly pass as athletic shorts when you're pantsless.

is for underwear.

Buy some new underwear. Something without revealing holes. Seriously. Because there are days—no, entire weekends—when it's all you'll wear. And you may not even notice it until you open the door on Sunday evening to get yesterday's paper and you feel a draft.

Don't pack. Rent. Most decent hotels and vacation properties rent everything from cribs to strollers at modest weekly prices. That will leave extra room for you to pack all your kick-ass Tommy Bahama shirts.

V

is for vacation.

Those hedonistic, whatever-shall-we-do-next, sex-at-any-time vacations are pretty much over. For now, at least. Now, it's more like how-the-hell-does-this-car-seat-fit-in-this-rental-car? Thailand is out, Florida is in. Late-night five-star dinners are replaced with the early-bird special so Baby can get home to bed. But trust me, inside of every new dad there's a Clark W. Griswold dying to get out. That first family vacation will prove it. You'll have the family loaded up and on the road to the Largest Ball of Twine in no time.

is for waistline.

As in 32. But now, 34. Next stop, housedress. There is no scientific link between the birth of your child and the absolute cold, hard stop of your metabolism. Yet. One theory suggests that men put on "sympathy weight" alongside their pregnant wife. But yet another theory suggests that nightly take-out, beer, and Baby Ruths eventually begin to make you fatter. It's simply too close to call. Don't worry; you'll eventually find time to hit the gym, bike, play video games, and do whatever you did before Baby came. Now you'll just do it with a trail of spit-up down the back of your shirt. You sexy MF.

You're going to be home a lot, up a lot, and bored a lot. And that means a lot of snacking. It's unavoidable. So just snack better. Try yogurt and granola, pretzels, even licorice. That way you can avoid craptastic light beer.

is for xylophone.

As in the little toy xylophone-on-wheels your parents have harbored in their basement since 1972. Sure, it's probably covered in toxic lead paint but, hey, it never harmed you, right? Debatable. Anyway, just smile and take it home. Parents like to believe there have been no significant advances in childcare for the last forty years. Your job is to make them believe they're right. So just lay your baby on the ultrasafe car floor mat when you pack up to leave, then switch her to that new-fangled "car seat" when your parents are out of sight.

Tell your parents what to do, finally. Sure, she's their grandchild, but she's your child. If you say no sweets, so be it. Hold them to it. Gray areas cause problems. They'll be wowed at their son's take-charge attitude.

is for yes.

Yes. You will take out the trash now. Yes. You will start the laundry. Yes. You will give the baby a bath. Yes. You will call the pediatrician at 3:21 A.M. Repeatedly. Yes. You will empty the diaper bin "before that smell makes me throw up." Yes. You will give the baby his medicine and if you don't know how much he gets you will "figure it out like a normal human being." Yes. You will resist the urge to complain and by doing so, you will become a bigger, better person and yes, it will be very, very worth it.

Get a laundry hamper with a removable netting for Baby's room. That makes it easy to lift out the whole load and dump it in the wash. And remember, use Dreft. Babies aren't ready for the hard stuff like you are, Mr. Badass.

"It's just a phase." The most important words in parenting. No matter what your kid is doing, it's just a phase. No matter how tiring it seems, it's just a phase. Things change. And get better. And then worse. And then better.